Disasters for All Time

THE CHALLENGER EXPLOSION

Valerie Bodden

CREATIVE EDUCATION • CREATIVE PAPERBACKS

Published by **Creative Education**
and **Creative Paperbacks**
P.O. Box 227, Mankato, Minnesota 56002

Creative Education and Creative Paperbacks
are imprints of **The Creative Company**
www.thecreativecompany.us

Design and production by **Joe Kahnke**
Art direction by **Rita Marshall**
Printed in China

Photographs by Alamy (SpaceX), Creative Commons Wikimedia (NASA), Flickr (NASA/Bill Ingalls, NASA/
Kim Shiflett, NASA Remix Man/NASA GRIN Archive), Getty Images (Bettmann, MPI/Stringer/Archive
Photos, Photo 12/Universal Images Group, Sovfoto/Universal Images Group), LostandTaken.com, NASA
(NASA, NASA/Bill Bowers/JSC, NASA/JSC, NASA/KSC, NASA/Michael O'Brien/JSC, NASA/MSFC), National
Archives and Records Administration (530679/Department of Defense), Newscom (Everett Collection),
Science Source (NASA/Bill Bowers), Shutterstock (Natasa Adzic)

Library of Congress Cataloging-in-Publication Data
Names: Bodden, Valerie, author. Title: The *Challenger* explosion / by Valerie Bodden.
Series: Disasters for all time. Includes index.

Summary: A historical account—including eyewitness quotes—of the devastating 1986 explosion of the space
shuttle *Challenger* and its effect on NASA's programs, ending with how the disaster is memorialized today.

Identifiers: LCCN 2017051377 / ISBN 978-1-64026-002-3 (hardcover)
/ ISBN 978-1-62832-547-8 (pbk) / ISBN 978-1-64000-021-6 (eBook)

Subjects: LCSH: 1. Challenger (Spacecraft)—Accidents—Juvenile literature. 2. Space vehicle accidents—
United States—Juvenile literature.

Classification: LCC TL867.B63 2018 / DDC 363.12/4—dc23

CCSS: RI.3.1-8; RI.4.1-5, 7; RI.5.1-3, 8; RI.6.1-2, 4, 7; RH.6-8.3-8

First Edition HC 9 8 7 6 5 4 3 2 1
First Edition PBK 9 8 7 6 5 4 3 2 1

CONTENTS

6

SHUTTLING INTO SPACE
Challenger Firsts - 15

16

A BUSY SCHEDULE
No Backup - 20

26

GO AT THROTTLE UP
Close Calls - 31

36

MOVING FORWARD
Space Tourism - 44

Glossary - 46   Read More / Websites - 47   Index - 48

1.28.

The morning of January 28, 1986, was unusually cold in Florida. People filled the stands at viewing sites near Kennedy Space Center. They were there to watch the launch of the space shuttle *Challenger*. It would be *Challenger*'s 10th launch into Earth orbit. It was the 25th mission of the United States' space shuttle program. But this launch was special. Along with six astronauts, the shuttle carried a teacher. Christa McAuliffe would be the first private citizen in space.

At 11:38 A.M., the shuttle's rockets roared to life. The shuttle lifted into the air. The crowds cheered as it rose higher. But 73 seconds after liftoff, there was an explosion. Smoke and fire surrounded the pieces of the shuttle. People in the crowd screamed. Then they fell silent. Some hoped the crew might have survived. But many at the National Aeronautics and Space Administration (NASA) knew this wasn't possible. There was no way to escape during the first two minutes of launch.

SHUTTLING INTO SPACE

The U.S. space program began in the late 1950s. During this time, the U.S. and the Soviet Union were engaged in the **Cold War**. The two countries built up their weapons stockpiles. They began a race to explore space. In 1957, the Soviet Union launched the first **satellite**. It showed the world that the country had rockets that could reach space. People worried that those same rockets could launch **nuclear** weapons to the U.S. The U.S. stepped up its own rocket program. It launched its first satellite in January 1958. But by then, the Soviet Union had already sent a dog into space.

In July 1958, NASA was formed. The agency focused on space science and exploration. It also started a program to put a person in space. But the Soviet Union beat NASA to it. On April 12, 1961, Soviet **cosmonaut** Yuri Gagarin rocketed into space. He became the first

7.20.1969

Apollo 11 reaches the moon

person to orbit Earth. Three weeks later, Alan Shepard became the first American in space. In February 1962, John Glenn was the first American to orbit Earth.

By then, president John F. Kennedy had set a new goal for the U.S. He wanted to put a man on the moon by 1970. NASA went to work. It created the Apollo spacecraft to reach the moon. But Project Apollo got off to a rough start. In January 1967, the Apollo 1 spacecraft sat on the launch pad. Three astronauts were inside for a preflight test. A fire ignited, killing all three.

Despite the tragedy, the Apollo program continued. On July 20, 1969, Apollo 11 reached the moon. Astronauts Neil Armstrong and Buzz Aldrin stepped onto the surface. The whole country celebrated. America had won the space race!

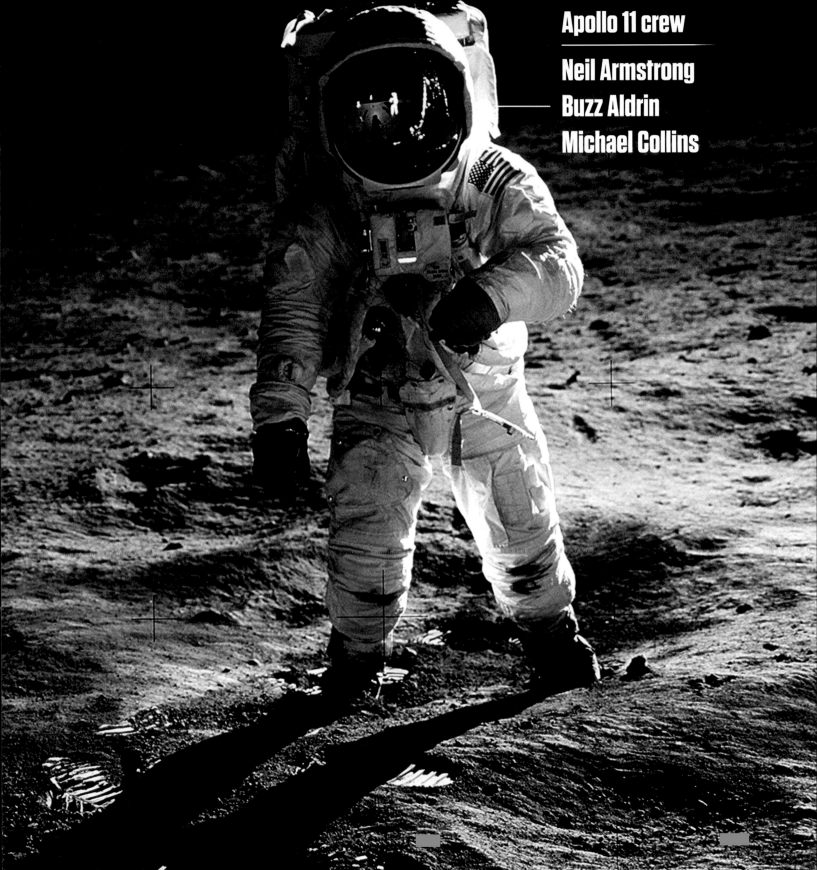

Apollo 11 crew

Neil Armstrong
Buzz Aldrin
Michael Collins

"I have decided today that the United States should proceed at once with the development of an entirely new type of space transportation system.... This system will center on a space vehicle that can shuttle repeatedly from Earth to orbit and back. It will revolutionize transportation into near space, by [making it routine]."

- President Richard Nixon, announcement of space shuttle program, 1972

Six more Apollo missions traveled to the moon. The last was Apollo 17. It reached the moon in 1972. President Richard Nixon set a new goal for NASA. He wanted the agency to build a reusable space shuttle. At first, plans also included a space station to orbit Earth. The shuttle would launch to the station. Someday, astronauts would travel from there to the moon and Mars. But NASA's budget was cut. The space station had to be set aside. Funding for the shuttle was cut in half.

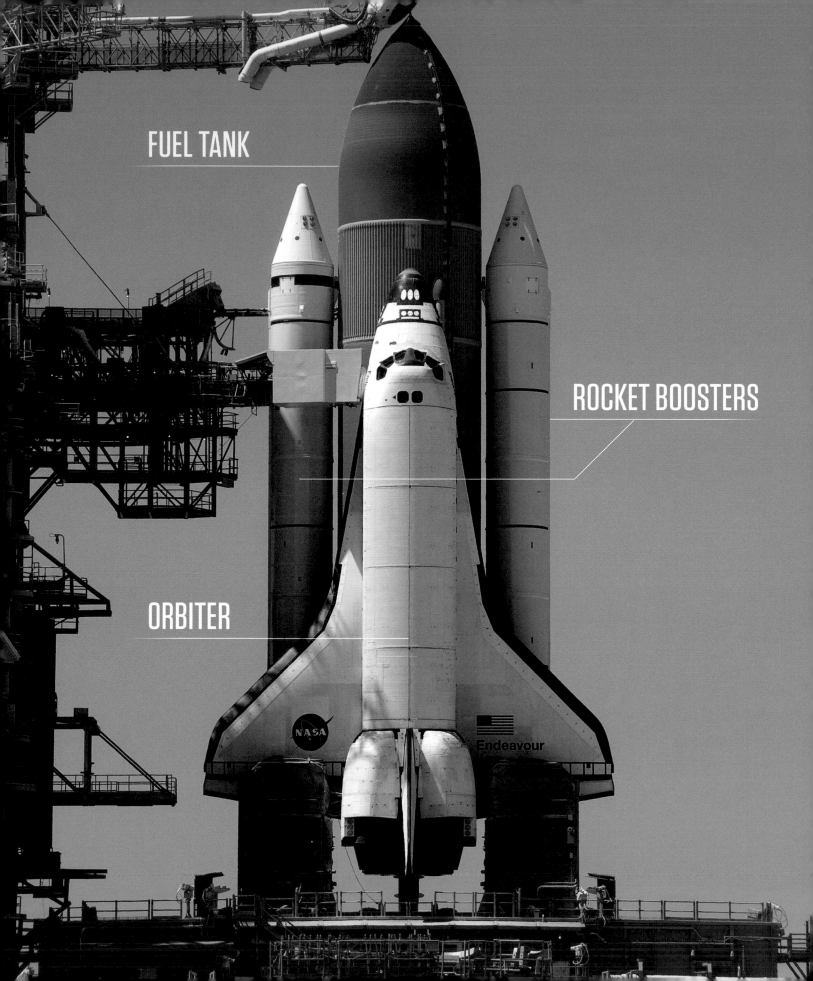

FUEL TANK

ROCKET BOOSTERS

ORBITER

NASA

Endeavour

NASA's design for the space shuttle included three parts. The orbiter was often referred to as the space shuttle. It looked like an airplane. It included the crew compartment and the cargo hold. The orbiter carried the crew back to Earth after a mission. It was attached to a huge external fuel tank. This orange tank carried fuel to power the shuttle's main engines. Once the fuel ran out, the tank was released. Two solid rocket boosters attached to the sides of the fuel tank. Each rocket was 150 feet (45.7 m) tall. They provided the lift needed to get the shuttle off the ground. Then they were dropped into the ocean. Each rocket booster had a

parachute. Ships pulled the rockets from the water so that they could be reused. Altogether, the shuttle weighed 5.4 million pounds (2.4 million kg). It could carry 65,000 pounds (29,484 kg) of cargo.

The first orbiter built for space flight was *Columbia*. On April 12, 1981, it traveled into orbit on a test flight. Two astronauts were aboard. They returned safely. *Columbia* went through three more test missions. Then NASA said the space shuttle was ready to go. Over the next four years, three more orbiters were built. They were named *Challenger*, *Discovery*, and *Atlantis*.

CHALLENGER FIRSTS

A number of space "firsts" happened on *Challenger* missions. The first spacewalk from a shuttle occurred on the *Challenger*. Sally Ride (pictured) became the first American woman in space aboard *Challenger*. Guion Bluford became the first African American in space aboard it. The orbiter was the first to be launched at night. It was the first to land at night, too. It was also the first to capture and repair a satellite.

II
A BUSY SCHEDULE

Each shuttle cost NASA millions of dollars to build and launch. The agency thought it could make some of this money back. It offered to take satellites into space for paying customers. The shuttle also carried satellites for the U.S. military. It hauled scientific instruments. And shuttle crews performed experiments in space.

To do all of this, NASA planned several shuttle launches each year. In 1985, the shuttles completed nine missions. Another 15 missions were scheduled for 1986. So many missions meant keeping to a tight schedule.

But the shuttles often had problems that caused delays. *Columbia* was supposed to launch in December 1985. But its flight was delayed seven times. It finally launched on January 12, 1986. Then its return was delayed for two days. That delay was caused by bad weather at the landing site. *Columbia* finally touched

Once satellites and other craft were in space, astronauts on shuttle missions in the 1980s often had to make repairs to them.

10 missions before STS-51-L

Pie chart 1 (17 launch attempts):
- 3 No Delay
- 4 Delayed <1 day
- 10 Delayed >1 day

Pie chart 2 (14 delays):
- 4 Weather
- 1 Other
- 9 Mechanical

down on January 18. *Challenger* was set to launch only eight days later.

High winds pushed the launch back two days. *Challenger* would not launch until January 28. The night before, the temperature at Kennedy Space Center dropped to 24 °F (-4.4 °C). Launch officials worried that pipes on the launch tower might freeze and burst. They let water drip out of the pipes to keep that from happening. The dripping water formed icicles on the tower. Some officials worried that the icicles would be knocked off during the launch. If the icicles hit the shuttle, they might damage its heat shield. This shield protected the orbiter from the massive heat that built up when it re-entered the **atmosphere** after a mission. Launch crews checked the icicles during the night and early morning. They removed as many as they could.

Before launches, NASA officials always checked in with the companies that had built the shuttle. The rockets

*Before **Challenger**'s very first flight, it was moved from the Vehicle Assembly Building to the launch pad in dense fog.*

NO BACKUP

NASA kept a list of items on the shuttle that had no backup system. If any of these failed, the shuttle would likely be lost. The list included nearly 750 items. In December 1982, the rocket boosters' O-rings were added to the list. **Engineers** at NASA and Morton Thiokol designed new O-rings. But replacing the O-rings would cause delays. NASA decided to keep the original parts.

were made by Morton Thiokol in Utah. Engineers there were worried. They had noticed problems with parts called O-rings. O-rings were thin rubber seals. They sat in joints between sections of the rockets. The seals were supposed to keep hot gases from burning through the steel motor case. But engineers had examined the O-rings on rockets from earlier shuttle flights. Some showed signs of wear. That wear was caused by hot gases. This meant the O-rings weren't sealing properly. Hot gases were getting past them. A second O-ring was supposed to serve as a backup if the primary O-ring failed. But the secondary O-ring sometimes moved out of position. In that case, the joint wouldn't seal at all.

The engineers worried that the problem would be worse in the cold. The cold would make the rubber O-rings stiffer. They might even be too stiff to seal. The

SOLID ROCKET

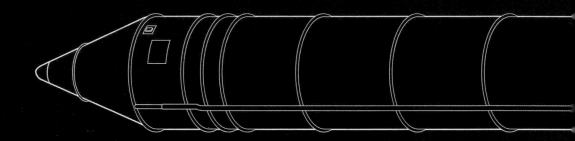

Nose Cap   Frustum   Forward Skirt   Forward Segment   Forward Mid Segment

O-rings

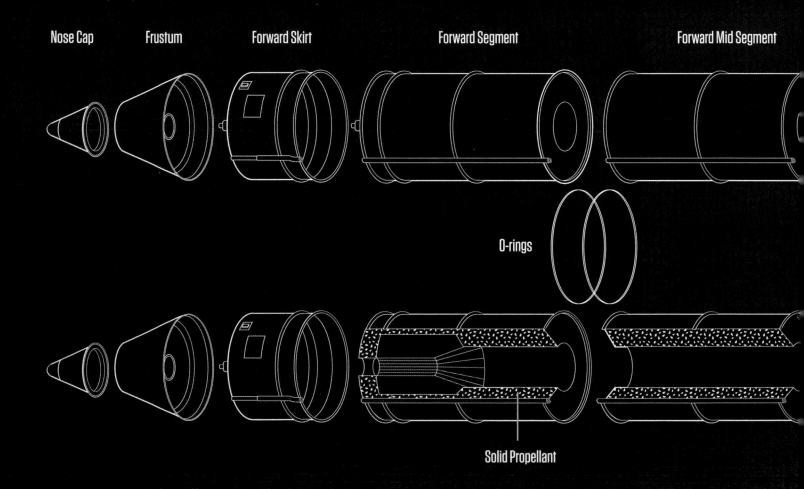

Solid Propellant

BOOSTER (SRB)

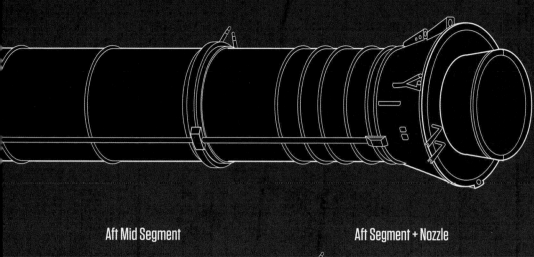

Aft Mid Segment   Aft Segment + Nozzle   Aft Skirt

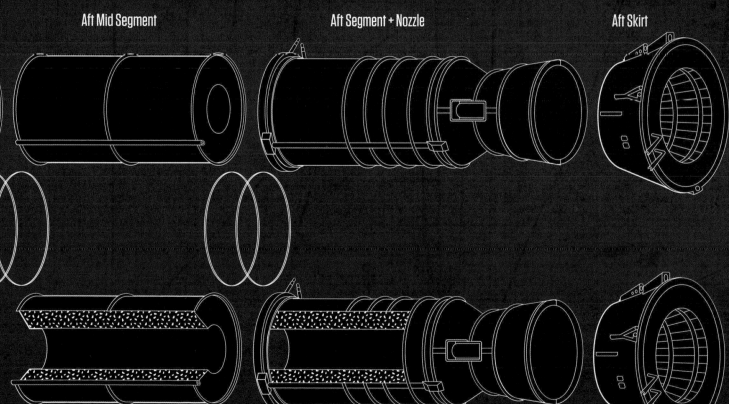

The coldest shuttle launch at 53 °F (11.7 °C) showed the worst O-ring damage yet. *Challenger* was set to launch under even colder conditions.

coldest shuttle launch had taken place the year before. *Discovery* had launched at 53 °F (11.7 °C). The O-rings from that mission had shown the worst damage yet. As temperatures dipped below freezing, Morton Thiokol engineers recommended that NASA delay *Challenger*'s launch.

They told this to officials at NASA's Marshall Space Flight Center in Alabama. The center was in charge of the rocket booster program. Marshall officials asked the engineers to prove the launch

wouldn't be safe. But they couldn't. The O-rings had never been tested in the cold. So managers at Morton Thiokol approved the launch. Launch directors at Kennedy Space Center were not told of the engineers' concerns about the O-rings. The *Challenger* crew didn't know, either.

Challenger's launch time was moved back an hour. This would allow more icicles to melt. But the mission was still go for launch.

"The result would be a catastrophe of the highest order—loss of human life…. It is my honest and very real fear that if we do not take immediate action to dedicate a team to solve the problem [of the O-rings], … then we stand in jeopardy of losing a flight, along with all the launch pad facilities."

Roger Boisjoly, Morton Thiokol engineer, memo to company management, July 1985

GO AT THROTTLE UP

The *Challenger* crew woke just after 6:00 A.M. on January 28. Francis "Dick" Scobee was the mission commander. Michael Smith would pilot the shuttle. Judith Resnik, Ronald McNair, and Ellison Onizuka would serve as mission specialists. Mission specialists were full-time astronauts. The mission also included two payload specialists. Payload specialists were trained for a specific mission. They were not full-time astronauts. Gregory Jarvis was an engineer. He would conduct experiments aboard the shuttle. Christa McAuliffe was a teacher. She would broadcast science lessons from space. The *Challenger* crew would also release a NASA satellite. They planned to set up an instrument to photograph Halley's Comet, too.

The crew enjoyed a breakfast of steak and eggs. Then they climbed into a van for the eight-mile (12.9 km)

Originally scheduled to launch on January 22, 1986, Challenger was delayed at least five times because of weather and scheduling problems.

Christa McAuliffe, a teacher from New Hampshire, was selected for the Challenger mission among more than 11,000 applicants.

drive to the launch pad. The sky was cloudless. Scobee commented on the nice weather.

At the launch pad, the crew rode the launch tower elevator. It carried them 195 feet (59.4 m) above the ground. They strapped on their helmets. Then they filed into the orbiter. Technicians helped buckle them in.

The crew waited as the countdown ticked toward liftoff. They knew that once the rockets lit, they could not escape for

THE CHALLENGER EXPLOSION

"I cannot join the space program and restart my life as an astronaut, but this opportunity to connect my abilities as an educator with my interests in history and space is a unique opportunity to fulfill my early fantasies. I watched the Space Age being born, and I would like to participate."

- Christa McAuliffe, application for Teacher in Space program, 1985

two minutes. The shuttle's designers had considered adding an emergency escape system. But design and budget limitations had ruled it out. Most rocket engineers thought the shuttle's rockets were the safest ever used. A launch escape system did not seem necessary.

After the first two minutes, the rockets would fall away. The shuttle's three main engines would power it for six more minutes. If an engine failed, the shuttle could release the tank. Then it could glide

to an emergency landing site. These sites were located in Florida, California, New Mexico, and Africa.

If everything went well, the shuttle would reach orbit eight and a half minutes after liftoff. The empty fuel tank would drop away. It would break up as it fell toward the ocean. The shuttle would orbit at 150 to 300 miles (241–483 km) above Earth. There it would travel at a speed of 17,000 miles (27,359 km) per hour. At this speed, a trip around the planet took only 90 minutes. After completing their mission, the crew would burn the shuttle's engine. This would take them out of orbit. They would re-enter Earth's atmosphere. An hour later, the orbiter would land at Kennedy Space Center.

With seven minutes left on the countdown, the crew lowered their helmet visors. At 15 seconds before liftoff, the main engines burst to life. Moments later, the solid rocket boosters fired. The shuttle

CLOSE CALLS

The space shuttle program had many close calls before the *Challenger* accident. A 1984 launch of *Discovery* was stopped four seconds before liftoff. A cracked valve in the engine had caused a small fire. In 1985, a *Challenger* launch was canceled. The orbiter had problems with the heat tiles. Later that year, one of *Challenger*'s main engines failed during liftoff. But the shuttle made it into orbit.

Just 73 seconds after liftoff, Challenger's right rocket booster failed, and the shuttle broke apart over the Atlantic Ocean.

Within 28 seconds, the shuttle was 10,000 feet (3,048 m) in the air. A minute after liftoff, it hit 35,000 feet (10,668 m).

lifted past the launch pad. To those on the ground, it seemed to move slowly. But within 28 seconds, the shuttle was 10,000 feet (3,048 m) in the air. A minute after liftoff, it hit 35,000 feet (10,668 m). It was now moving at a rate of 2,900 feet (884 m) per second.

NASA controllers monitored the launch from the Mission Control Center in Houston, Texas. Everything seemed normal to both the shuttle crew and the controllers. At one minute and seven seconds, mission control said to continue at full throttle, or full speed. Scobee reported back, "Roger, go at throttle up." That was the last thing mission control heard from the crew.

Seconds later, mission control lost all data from the shuttle. Cameras showed it breaking up in a ball of flame. It was 50,800 feet (15,484 m) above Earth. That is more than 9.6 miles (15.4 km). Pieces continued to shoot upward. Some parts reached an **altitude** of 122,000 feet (37,186 m). Then they rained down into the sea.

Engine exhaust, a plume from the SRB, and a ball of gas from the external tank were visible within seconds.

CHALLENGER EXPLOSION
Timeline

1:35 A.M. — Ice inspection crew removes icicles from the launch pad site.

6:00 A.M. — *Challenger* crew awakes and eats steak and eggs for breakfast.

8:03 A.M. — The crew arrives at the launch pad and rides the elevator up the launch tower.

8:44 A.M. — A second ice inspection is completed.

11:31 A.M. — The crew lowers their helmet visors.

11:38 A.M. — The shuttle's rockets ignite for liftoff. Crowds cheer.

+58 SEC — A flame flickers from the right solid rocket booster.

+15 SEC — The shuttle explodes.

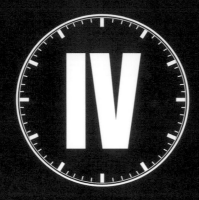

IV

MOVING FORWARD

People around the world mourned the *Challenger* crew. Many had seen the accident live on TV. Some thought it meant the end of the U.S. space program.

On January 31, NASA held a memorial service at Johnson Space Center in Texas. More than 10,000 people attended. Thousands more watched on TV. President Ronald Reagan gave a speech. He promised that the space program would continue.

But all shuttle flights were grounded. President Reagan appointed a group to investigate the accident. The group was known as the Rogers Commission. It included Neil Armstrong, the first man on the moon. It also included Sally Ride, the first American woman in space.

NASA officials pored over films of the launch. They presented their findings to the Rogers Commission.

After the disaster, President Reagan accompanied family members of the Challenger crew at a memorial service in Texas.

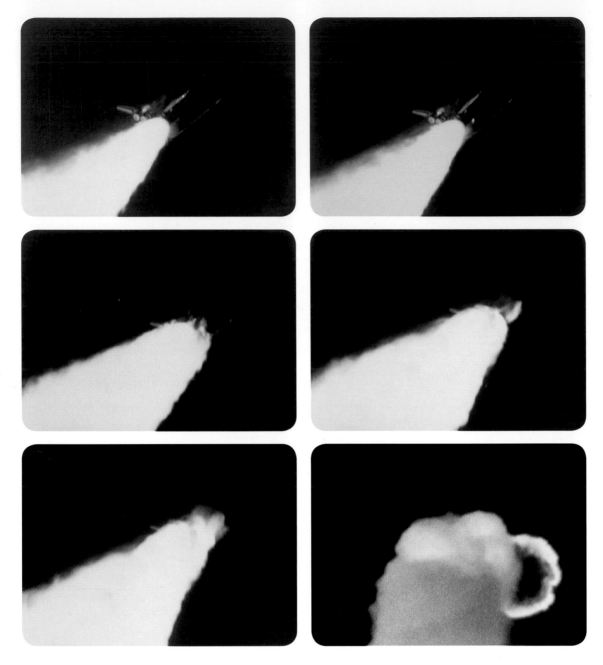

The films showed a puff of smoke coming off a joint of the right rocket booster. The smoke soon turned into a glow of fire. It spread along the fuel tank. Officials realized that hot gas had likely gotten past the O-rings. It burned through the spot where the bottom of the rocket attached to the fuel tank. This made the rocket's nose swing forward. The rocket crashed into the fuel tank, causing the explosion. Debris pulled from the ocean proved NASA's theory. Parts of the right rocket booster had been burned through.

The Rogers Commission released its

"We've grown used to wonders in this century. It's hard to dazzle us. But for 25 years the United States space program has been doing just that. We've grown used to the idea of space, and perhaps we forget that we've only just begun. We're still pioneers. They, the members of the Challenger crew, were pioneers."

President Ronald Reagan, address to the nation, January 28, 1986

ISS Tranquility node 3

Cargo bay

Endeavour

report on June 6, 1986. The report blamed the design of the rocket joint for the accident. It faulted both NASA and Morton Thiokol for not fixing the problem with the O-rings. The commission learned that both organizations had known about the issue. As a result of the report, several safety issues on the shuttle were improved. The seal on the rocket boosters was changed.

Thirty-two months after the *Challenger*

accident, a shuttle stood on the launch pad again. On September 29, 1988, *Discovery* launched. Space shuttle flights continued. The orbiter *Endeavour* was built to replace *Challenger*. The shuttle program no longer carried satellites for paying customers. Instead, shuttle missions focused on military and scientific projects. In 1998, shuttles began to carry parts of the **International Space Station** (ISS) into orbit. The shuttle's robotic arm helped

Endeavour *flew 25 successful missions, retiring after it delivered yet more components to the ISS in 2011.*

assemble the parts. Astronauts began staying on the station in November 2000.

Soon, shuttle launches seemed almost routine. But on February 1, 2003, disaster struck again. The space shuttle *Columbia* broke apart during re-entry. All seven crew members died. A piece of foam from the fuel tank had fallen off during takeoff. It damaged the orbiter's heat shield. The next shuttle didn't fly until July 2005. By then, the end of the shuttle program was in sight. The final shuttle mission returned to Earth on July 21, 2011.

The end of the shuttle program did not mean the end of space travel. Astronauts continued to live on the ISS. They reached it aboard Russian Soyuz spacecraft. **Commercial** rockets carried supplies to the station.

NASA also began to look beyond the ISS. It began building a new spacecraft called Orion.

All seven members aboard Columbia *died when the shuttle re-entered Earth's atmosphere after completing a 16-day mission in 2003.*

SPACE TOURISM

One of the purposes of sending a teacher into space was to open space travel to the wider public. That vision is carried out today by private companies. They are working to develop space tourism. Virgin Galactic planned to send tourists on a **suborbital** flight in 2018. SpaceX plans to launch two tourists around the moon. Space tourists have already visited the ISS. They traveled aboard Russian Soyuz craft.

A piece of Challenger's *fuselage and other debris are part of a permanent exhibit called "Forever Remembered" at Kennedy Space Center.*

The spacecraft would travel farther into space than humans had ever gone. NASA set a goal of landing humans on Mars in the 2030s.

As NASA looks to the future of space travel, it remembers the crew of the *Challenger*. Kennedy Space Center exhibits an astronaut memorial. It pays tribute to all who have died in space exploration. It includes personal items from the crews of *Challenger* and *Columbia*. It displays pieces of the two shuttles. The exhibit reminds visitors of the losses of the past. But it also directs them toward the promise of the future.

GLOSSARY

altitude the height of an object above Earth's surface

atmosphere the layer of gases surrounding Earth or another planet

Cold War a period of rivalry after World War II between the communist Soviet Union and the democratic United States

commercial having to do with business and the selling of goods or services

cosmonaut an astronaut from the Soviet Union (later Russia)

Earth orbit a path around Earth followed by an object in space

engineers people who use math and science to design and build machines, roads, buildings, and other structures

International Space Station an artificial structure that orbits Earth and provides life support systems for astronauts who often remain aboard for several months and conduct scientific experiments

nuclear powered by energy made by the fusing or splitting of atoms

satellite an artificial object that orbits a planet or moon and collects information to send back to Earth

suborbital describing a flight that does not complete a full orbit around Earth

READ MORE

Royston, Angela. *Space*. Mankato, Minn.: Smart Apple Media, 2016.

Stone, Adam. *The Challenger Explosion*. Minneapolis: Bellwether Media, 2014.

WEBSITES

NASA for Students
https://www.nasa.gov/audience/forstudents/index.html

Learn more about NASA's programs and history.

NASA: High Definition Earth-Viewing System
https://eol.jsc.nasa.gov/ESRS/HDEV/

Check out the live view of Earth from the International Space Station.

Note: Every effort has been made to ensure that any websites listed above were active at the time of publication. However, because of the nature of the Internet, it is impossible to guarantee that these sites will remain active indefinitely or that their contents will not be altered.

INDEX

Aldrin, Buzz 8

Armstrong, Neil 8, 36

Bluford, Guion 15

Boisjoly, Roger 25

Gagarin, Yuri 6, 8

Glenn, John 8

Halley's Comet 26

International Space Station 40, 42, 44

Jarvis, Gregory 26

Kennedy, John F. 8

McAuliffe, Christa 4, 26, 29

McNair, Ronald 26

Morton Thiokol 20, 21, 24, 25, 40

NASA 4, 5, 6, 8, 10, 13, 14, 16, 18, 20, 24, 26,
        30, 33, 36, 38, 40, 42, 45
    formation of 6
    Johnson Space Center 36
    Kennedy Space Center 4, 18, 24, 30, 45
    and Mars goals 10, 45
    Marshall Space Flight Center 24
    Mission Control Center 33
    Orion spacecraft 42, 45
    Project Apollo 8, 10, 36
        moon landings 8, 10, 36
        spacecraft 8, 10

Nixon, Richard 10

Onizuka, Ellison 26

Reagan, Ronald 36, 39

Resnik, Judith 26

Ride, Sally 15, 36

Rogers Commission 36, 38, 40

Russia 6, 42, 44
    and Cold War 6
    Soyuz spacecraft 42, 44

satellites 6, 15, 16, 26, 40

Scobee, Francis "Dick" 26, 28, 33

Shepard, Alan 8

Smith, Michael 26

space shuttles 4–5, 10, 13, 14, 15, 16, 18, 20,
        21, 24, 25, 26, 28–29, 30, 31, 33, 35, 36,
        38, 39, 40, 42, 45
    Atlantis 14
    Challenger 4–5, 14, 15, 18, 24, 26, 30,
        31, 35, 36, 39, 40, 45
    Columbia 14, 16, 18, 42, 45
    delays 16, 18, 20, 24, 31
    Discovery 14, 24, 31, 40
    and emergency landing sites 30
    Endeavour 40
    fuel tanks 13, 29, 30, 38, 42
    O-rings 20, 21, 24, 25, 38, 40
    solid rocket boosters 5, 13, 14, 20, 21, 24,
        28, 29, 30, 35, 38, 40

space tourism 44
    SpaceX 44
    Virgin Galactic 44